D1391936

Telling Tales

Telling Tales

Alan Bennett

BOOKS

The photograph on page 2 is by Stephen Morley, © Slow Motion Ltd.
All other photographs courtesy Alan Bennett.

The quotations from poems by Philip Larkin are reproduced by kind
permission of the following: The Marvell Press for 'I Remember,
I Remember' from *The Less Deceived*; Faber and Faber Ltd for 'The Building'
from *High Windows*.

First published in hardback 2000 and in paperback 2001
This edition published by BBC Books an imprint of Ebury Publishing
A Random House Group Company

The Random House Group Limited Reg. No. 954009
Addresses for companies within the Random House Group can be found at
www.randomhouse.co.uk

A CIP catalogue record for this book is available from the British library.

ISBN 978 1846 072 604

The Random House Group Limited makes every effort to ensure that the
papers uded in our books are made from trees that have been legally sourced
from well-managed and credibly certified forests. our paper procurement
policy can be found at www.randomhouse.co.uk

Commissioning editors: Emma Shackleton and Martin Redfern
Project editor: Martha Caute
Designer: Linda Blakemore

Printed and bound in Italy by LegoPrint S.p.A.

CONTENTS

INTRODUCTION

TELLING A TALE, certainly in the north of England, can mean telling a lie; and telling the tale means a story told at unnecessary length, 'telling t' tale from t' thread to t' needle' a narrative packed with redundant information. Telling tales is also, of course, sneaking, a way of passing on information best kept to yourself. If, as I'm sure, all these are charges that can be levelled against my *Telling Tales*, then at least it means I've got the title right.

It's true also that a telling tale can be a tale that carries weight, a tale with implications. Whether that applies I am less certain.

Since I've written two previous series of monologues for television, it's natural to assume that these ten pieces, all for one voice, are another exercise in the same form. This would be wrong, as none of these pieces has plot or drama; they do not conceal information as the other monologues do, nor, I hope, does the narrator play tricks. Besides, the tales told here are true.

Get to my age, and you are often asked to take part in radio or television programmes of reminiscence, looking back on your own life or the lives and careers of former colleagues. Celebrations, they are currently called, which, festive though it sounds, also strikes the posthumous note. So anxious are we to be positive, that these days memorial services and even funerals are advertised as celebrations. If I tend to give such television or radio programmes a wide berth, it's not on account of this prevailing whiff of mortality. Nor is it modesty that deters me, though it often strikes me (struck me particularly after Peter Cook's death) that to pass judgement on the dead, however favourably, is a form of condescension and often of self-advertisement. No, if I'm honest, what makes me give such programmes the thumbs down is sheer self-interest; I resent handing over my memories without being properly compensated for them.

When *Omnibus*, say, or the *South Bank Show* break it to you that you might be the subject of an in-depth study, before being too flattered it's as well to remember that such programmes, and the similar but less prestigious compilations that infest the sillier channels, are above all cheap – film clips are not hard to come by, ex-colleagues are only too eager to assess and reminisce and, of course, the cheapest and most useful property is yourself, the subject of the programme. For a nominal fee you divest yourself of memories, anecdotes and all the accumulated baggage of years and, in effect, put on an extended and, you hope, entertaining turn on the subject of your life.

Much of what I've written in *Telling Tales* could have been told to an interviewer – to Melvyn Bragg, say, or in an *Omnibus* film, to a voice off camera that is less endowed with personality. It could also be done on a chat show. Probed by the caring, maieutic voice of the interviewer, you regurgitate with a fetching spontaneity recollections you have already recollected for some nervous young researcher beforehand, the most intimate moments of your life now the sport of a studio audience.

It's an exercise that is in every sense of the word profitless and costive by nature. I've come to see it as not only distasteful but squandering. If there are any tales to be told, then I want to tell them, and tell them unmediated.

This disaffection applies, too, to newspaper interviews, which I've grown to dislike more and more over the years. Journalists seldom get it right and, even when accurately reporting one's words, don't catch the tone in which they're said, cutting out the qualifications (and I am all qualifications), pruning away the halts and hesitations, so that what comes across is a creature more lucid and loquacious than I could hope (or want) to be. Equipped though you may be with readily unsheathed opinions or primed with impressive generalisations, you nevertheless end up seeming a clown. And, like Kingsley Amis saying he no longer did dinners, so one of life's late joys for me is finding I don't have to do interviews. If there is anything to be said, I prefer to say it myself; probing will have to wait.

Still, it's reassuring to be asked about your life if only because it makes you feel you've had one – though, as Flannery O'Connor wrote, 'Anyone who has survived childhood has enough information to last him the rest of his days.' The risk, of course, of telling tales on television, particularly about a childhood in the north, is that you may end up writing an extended Hovis commercial.

Still, it's reassuring to be asked about your life if only because it makes you feel you've had one.

Though my childhood was, I suppose, happy, I do not see it bathed in the golden light or tinted that dusty sepia (with trumpet obbligato) in which such epics are shot. I see it as dull now as I saw it as dull then; safe too, and above all ordinary. Which, if pressed to locate themselves on the social scale, is what my parents would say they were: not working class, certainly not middle class, but ordinary.

Though my childhood was, I suppose, happy, I do not see it bathed in the golden light or tinted that dusty sepia (with trumpet obbligato) ...

In many ways, though, they were not ordinary at all and certainly not typical. My father had no time for sport, for instance, football, particularly on television, being the bane of his life. 'Stinking football,' he used to say then, though what he would make of today's soccer-soaked schedules I daren't think. Without being at all pious, neither of them touched alcohol, which limited their social life. He disliked all male company as my mother did the exclusive company of women and they were happiest – only happy really – when together. They were shy, timorous, silly and full of fun, and they were, as I hope these tales show, far from ordinary if by that one means commonplace.

Even so, a sense of being different isn't something they relished, so that being ordinary was a state to which they almost aspired. They had a longing to be ordinary – or at least like other people – and not to be perceived as different or set apart. Hence Dad's joy when so late in the day he passes his driving test, or Mam's excitement, seeing their social life about to improve, when she telephones me to say that they have at last discovered an alcoholic drink they like. 'It's called bitter lemon.'

... being ordinary was a state to which they most aspired.

As with drink so with snapshots. Though each story begins with a photograph, generally a family snap, taking pictures in our family is a far from routine occurrence, usually because there is not much to take pictures of. My brother and I growing up is the most regular subject, and what pictures of places there are, even when the place is out of the ordinary, are only a background to that. There survive, for instance, only two photographs of us at Byril Farm, where we were evacuated, one, shown at the start of 'Our War' with the four of us on a farm cart and Mr Weatherhead between the shafts, the other of my brother and me (as ever, in our school caps) sitting on Tommy the horse in the orchard. Though there is a photograph of the Weatherheads themselves, with their wonderful Dales faces, it's taken at a proper photographer's in Harrogate – whereas my remembrance is of Mrs Weatherhead churning butter or going out in an old raincoat to feed the hens and clattering the cockerels with the feed bucket when they fly up in her face.

Our snaps are never labelled or find their way into an album and, one breakwater looking very much like another, it's hard now to decide whether it's Filey we're paddling at or Redcar or Caton Bay, and it's only the look of Gordon and me that gives a notion of the date.

Our snaps are never labelled or find their way into an album.

Though he may seem happy in these early photographs, Dad grows to dislike having his picture taken, at the sight of a camera his face taking on a long-suffering look reminiscent of Somerset Maugham during his last days at the Villa Mauresque. 'Don't pull your jib,

Dad,' Mam mutters, but in middle age he seldom manages to look other than pissed off. I suspect that the photo taken of him in his Otley Road shop, which concludes the television version of 'A Shy Butcher', must have been taken by a customer to whom he has to be polite, as it's one of the few photographs before his retirement where he looks relatively cheerful.

In several of these seaside snapshots in the thirties, Dad is wearing his bowler hat even when sitting in a deckchair on the sands. The shot of the four of us, which kicks off 'A Strip of Blue' and which must be dated some time in 1938, is notable in that it's the last time the bowler puts in an appearance. For

... Dad is wearing his bowler hat even when sitting in a deckchair on the sands.

some reason other than fashion, expense possibly, the bowler is an early casualty of the war and henceforth and for the next thirty years it will always be a trilby.

Too old to catch the camera habit themselves, my parents do not pass it on to me and I still seldom think to take a camera with me, though if I did I would perhaps be an even less assiduous diarist than I am. I am no more fond of my face than my father was of his, and that, too, is a deterrent to taking photographs, as having no children (or pets) is another.

The paucity of family photographs can also be put down to the war when film was hard to come by. Nor was it cheap, coming in rolls of eight or twelve, with the changing of the roll always a fiddling business. The notion that photographs are a resource to be used sparingly persists with me even into the sixties, and one of the amazements attendant on *Beyond the Fringe* in 1961 and my first whiff of celebrity, is how recklessly smart photographers like Cecil Beaton and Lewis Morley (though not Bill Brandt) run off roll after roll of film, expense plainly no object. I think back to our meagre output of half a dozen snaps a year and realise this must be life.

Conscious that, like the childhood they recount, my memories are unstartling, I find no comfort in the knowledge that others have felt the same. Notable among them is Philip Larkin, whose poem *I Remember, I Remember* tells of finding himself on a train that stops unexpectedly at Coventry.

> 'Why Coventry!' I exclaimed. 'I was born here.'
> I leant far out, and squinnied for a sign
> That this was still the town that had been 'mine'

So long, but found I wasn't even clear
Which side was which.

Even to quote Larkin is to feel that anything I have
said has been (un)said already and that his grumpy
particularities far outsay my own. Elsewhere, he
describes his childhood as 'a forgotten boredom,' and
that, too, I endorse – the whole of *Telling Tales* an
expansion both on Larkin's phrase 'how my childhood was unspent' and (the concluding line of *I
Remember, I Remember*) 'Nothing, like something,
happens anywhere.'

It seems like nothing happening at the time too;
life is elsewhere and one of the incentives to get away
to university is just to be
somewhere else and lead
the life and see the places I
read about in books. Leeds
and a childhood in Leeds
do not figure in any of the
books I read, the provinces
still – well – provincial. The

*Leeds and a child-
hood in Leeds
do not figure in
any of the books
I read ...*

first time I come across a childhood anything like my
own is in Richard Hoggart's *The Uses of Literacy*. But
even this isn't like my childhood – the poverty more

dire, the neighbourhood (Hunslet) poorer than Armley and the Hoggart family more rugged and deprived than the Bennetts ever succeeded in being.

By this time, though, my childhood is over, just when the kind of upbringing I have had (or a less watered-down version of it) is starting to be written about in novels and plays, and even to be seen at the cinema and on the stage of the Royal Court. Had I known it was going to become fashionable I might have enjoyed it more – or at least taken more notice when it was happening. So it was another bus I felt I had missed.

Had I known it was going to become fashionable I might have enjoyed it more …

The television programmes were recorded over a period of five days on Stage 2 at Ealing, our little set islanded in a vast hangar that had seen grander days. I made myself familiar with the text without quite knowing it by heart and used a tele-prompter. This shows occasionally, I think, when the delivery sometimes gets too assured (or too assured for me). My natural mode is one of hesitancy and repetition which, over a period of time, would have become irritating to the viewer; I couldn't have just talked the programmes through. In reading the script it's hard, though, to keep out of one's voice a slightly rhetorical tone, a feeling that you are not in conversation but are addressing some sort of gathering (if not quite the nation).

The programmes were directed by Patrick Garland and Tristram Powell, with both of whom I've worked before. It's easy to distinguish who did what as I tend to wring my hands when talking, a habit Patrick didn't mind or try to keep out of shot; Tristram, perhaps through working at the same time on a hard-nosed police series, preferred a less anguished mode, so in his monologues there is no hand-wringing.

I've also recorded these talks (a nice old-fashioned description) for radio, which would seem their obvious medium, but as with the two series of *Talking Heads*, I wanted to do them on television first, if only because they make more demands on the viewer than they do the listener. Talking to camera is hardly a form I can be said to have invented, but just as the first series of *Talking Heads* was followed by other sequences of monologues so, I imagine, *Telling Tales* will have its imitators and for the same reasons, namely, that it's a form that is seemingly simple to do and (an over-whelming argument nowadays) cheap.

A final word on writing about parents, again from Flannery O'Connor: 'I once had the feeling I would dig my mother's grave with my writing but I later discovered this was vanity on my part. They are hardier than we think.'

Alan Bennett

A Strip of Blue

Telling Tales

WHEN HOLBEIN'S *A Lady with a Squirrel and a Starling* came to the National Gallery in 1993, it was taken out of its frame for technical examination and, where it had been protected from the light by the frame, there was revealed a strip of blue paint as fresh and bright as when it had been put on by Holbein more than four and a half centuries ago.

There were no Holbeins at 12 Halliday Place, the house in Armley, Leeds, where I was born and brought up, but in our deserted front room, the sitting room as I suppose it should have been called and which in 1941 was uncarpeted and almost unfurnished, there was a sofa, the surviving member of a three-piece suite bought at the Co-op in October 1928, a few weeks after my parents got married. The suite cost £26 15s 6d, the bill still there among my father's few papers when he died nearly fifty years later.

This sofa has originally been upholstered in blue and bronze embossed velour, but bleached by the sun pouring through the bay window (though latterly somewhat shaded by the air-raid shelter that stands in the street outside), the sofa has weathered over the years to a lumpy donkeyish grey. My brother and I play on it, our particular delight to let down the end arm, a lever in the side allowing you to do this with satisfying suddenness. Once down, the arm reveals, as it might be the Holbein, a strip of unsunned, unworn upholstery with its original bronze and azure colours as bright and unfaded as they must have been in the first weeks of my parents' marriage.

As a child of seven I look on this small strip of pristine colour with wonder, taking its undimmed blue and bronze to be a glimpse of what life had been like in that, to me, legendary period Before the War – and when my parents were just married. Because it was certainly different. The photographs of holidays at Filey when I am still a baby show Mam young and carefree and prettier than she is now. Dad, in bathing costume, holds up Gordon to the camera, smiling, unworried, but above all *there*: on our holidays during the war he seldom is, not because he's been called up but more prosaically always has to go back to Leeds after a couple of days to mind the Co-op butcher's shop he manages in Armley Lodge Road.

The photographs of holidays at Filey when I am still a baby show Mam young and carefree and prettier than she is now.

So this unfaded riband of blue and gold seems to me like a bright flag that has been lowered on a regime that we shall never see again. I am seven or eight at this time and already halfway to believing that we have had the best of it.

On the bill from the Co-op Furnishing Department is our dividend number, 105219, a number learned by heart by us as children as soon as we are old enough to be sent shopping at the Co-op on Ridge Road. It is one of a trio of numbers I will never forget until I forget everything, the others being 51879, our first telephone number, and 2270017, my army number, for any of which I would unthinkingly put up my hand were they called out even to select me for death.

> *It is one of a trio of numbers I will never forget until I forget everything.*

It is at No. 12 Halliday Place, three years after they are married, that my brother is born on 9 May 1931. And on the same date, 9 May, but three years later I arrive, both of us born at home in the bed which figures on the Co-op bill and which cost £4 4s. We must have been conceived in the rather less cosy surroundings of a boarding-house bedroom as, counting back, our conceptions occur, rather sadly I always feel, during the August Bank Holiday, one of those carefree pre-war holidays of which I still have a few snaps.

My birth is easier than my brother's, during which my mother's screams can be heard right down the street, and there are still scratches at the foot of the bed claimed by my mother to have been made by her toe-nails during the long hours it took for my

brother to be born. I find this difficult to believe, though I would like it to be the case, as the bed is the bed in which I still sleep. Comfortable enough, it's not a particularly pleasing piece of furniture and currently I'm thinking of painting it some more fashionable shade, but what deters me are those fabled and almost archaeological scratches.

Though the first ten years of my life are spent at No. 12 Halliday Place, our house is far less vivid in memory than the more constricted surroundings of my Grandma's. Her back-to-back house is in Gilpin Place in Wortley and, bizarrely, what brings it back most vividly is the smell of mimosa, dry and a touch musty and used as backing for the weekend flowers. I have no notion as a child of mimosa as something exotic and think of it as a weed almost until going abroad for the first time at the age of twenty, and hitchhiking near Cahors under a baking sun I catch a powerful swig of it from a neighbouring field and am instantly back in the sooty back streets of Wortley and Grandma's front room with the flowers in the celery glass on the piano.

As children we can chart the subtlest differences between the streets and the houses in the streets. We know that Grandma's house, 7 Gilpin Place, is slightly superior to the one next door because it's the end house and so handier for the yard with the outside lavatories. Grandma's house is superior too on account of its tiny patch of sooty grass, a lawn so small it accommodates our tent but not its guy ropes, their aluminium pegs having to be thrust between the paving stones of the path or plugged into the brickwork of the cellar window. It is a feat of construction as ingenious in its way as the tent I marvel to see erected thirty years later on the stage of the Royal Court in Lindsay Anderson's production of David Storey's play *The Contractor*.

As children we know both in Armley and Wortley the streets that are safe to go along – no rough children, no big dogs, no mad people or tramps. Traffic, of course, doesn't come into it as there is none anywhere. Most children will carry such maps in their heads and these days when living in cities is a more perilous business than it was these personal topographies have a name: it's called being street-wise which, as a child, threading my timorous way through the close-packed red brick acres, neat, cautious and fearful, I am by instinct.

Traffic, of course, doesn't come into it as there is none anywhere.

At the top house opposite Grandma's live a tramdriver and his wife, Edna, who is always ill and thought to be dying. We are told to pray for her, which I do conscientiously well into the fifties, when she is still alive and still presumably dying, but by then she has outlived most of the street.

So Edna for me is a name that is redolent of suffering and now, of course, a name from the past, the name of the kind of character I all too often find myself writing about – ageing aunties, denizens of retirement homes, old people on their last legs, the personnel very often of the kind of streets I have been recalling and whose idiom and way of talking and thinking derived from living in such streets. So when such characters have to be denominated, the occupants of the cots in old people's homes given names, I choose them from suitably old-fashioned stock – Frank, Harold, Alice, Nora – names of the period.

Except that the personnel of these geriatric scrapheaps is beginning to alter. Ranged in vacant rooms or stood immobilised by a radiator, these shrunken creatures still answer to Hannah, Arthur, Peggy or Bill. And one of the ways the young think they are safeguarded against the fate and future of their grandparents is by their names: Sharons don't suffer from dementia or Damians from incontinence. And if the old ones can think at all, they must wonder if their names are part of the trouble. They've been called the wrong thing, that's what's the matter. With names like Frank or Norman, Ernest or Gilbert, they're already weighted in the direction of the grave.

Jeremys don't fail as they have failed. Piss doesn't trickle unheeded down a Nicky's leg. And if a Darren dies it's in a motorway pile-up, not in a sunshine home. But not for much longer.

And if a Darren dies it's in a motor-way pile-up not in a sunshine home. But not for much longer.

Soon the listless watchers by the radiator will be Melanie and Karen, Lee and Sandra-Louise. The trumpet has not yet sounded for Trevor but it will. In a TV play of mine called *Rolling Home* there is a scene in which the middle-aged children of a father dead in an old people's home are coming away, carrying his meagre possessions just as the matron is helping a new arrival, another old man, out of the ambulance. 'Hello,' she says brightly. 'Welcome: you're our first Kevin!'

They're cheaper names now, the new ones, fluorescent, names fit for name tags and laminating on plastic, not to be carved in stone or inscribed by a proper signwriter as the old names were. You can dissolve them these new names, sponge them away, whereas my Grandma's name, Mary Ann Peel, was marked on every cell of her body.

Of course, some names will not seem to change at all. There are Joes in homes and Joes in playgroups and Jacobs too, and though it will take a lifetime, the young Joes and Jacobs will in due course come along to take their namesakes' places, shuffling the dominoes, gazing vacantly at a plate of mince.

There will be new Hannahs too, Emilys, though the second wave of Emilys will come from higher up the social scale, just as an old Jacob is not the same as a new Jacob, and not just because the new Jacob prefers to be called Jake. The old Jacob, like the old Joseph, was shabby and vaguely biblical. The new Jacob is secular and smart; the name has been sanded down and all its biblical varnish gone.

Some names will not come round again. The Dorises are going, for instance, and the Hildas and how many boys now get called my father's name, Walter? One can just about imagine a baby called Mabel but who would turn out the name drawer to christen their child Edna? But coming up

One can just about imagine a baby called Mabel but who would turn out the name drawer to christen their child Edna?

the road are the Deans and the Darrens and the
Waynes and they too shall fail; it won't be long before
even Tiffany is a grandmother and her cot got ready
in the corner. Her children, middle aged and vaguely
resentful, come and sit with her on Sunday afternoons
while she tries to remember who they are and who
she is. 'You're Tiffany, Mother. And this is your little
grand-daughter.'

And what will her name be?

Our War

TO BE BROUGHT UP IN LEEDS in the forties was to learn early on the quite useful lesson that life is generally something that happens elsewhere. It is true that I was around in time for the Second World War but so far as Leeds was concerned that was certainly something that happened elsewhere. From time to time the sirens went and my brother and I were wrapped in blankets and hustled out to the air-raid shelter that stood outside our suburban front door, there to await the longed-for rain of bombs. Sheffield caught it, Liverpool caught it, but Leeds, it seemed, hardly ever. 'Why should it? I live here,' was my reasoning, though there was a more objective explanation. The city specialised in the manufacture of ready-made suits and the culti-vation of rhubarb and, though the war aims of the German High Command were notoriously quixotic, I imagine a line had to be drawn somewhere. Thus, in the whole course of hostilities, only a handful of bombs fell on Leeds, most of which did little damage and were promptly torn apart by schoolboys, famished for shrapnel.

Sheffield caught it, Liverpool caught it but Leeds, it seemed, hardly ever.

I am five when the war starts and Monday, September 4th 1939, should be my first day at school; but this is not to be. I wish I could record my family as gathered anxiously round the wireless, as most were at eleven o'clock that Sunday morning, but I already know at the age of five that I belong to a family that, without being in the least bit remarkable or eccentric, yet manages never to be quite like other families. If we had been, then my brother and I would have been evacuated with all the other children the week before, but Mam and Dad haven't been able to face it. So, not quite partaking in the national mood and, as ever, unbrushed by the wings of history, Mr Chamberlain's broadcast finds us on a tram going down Tong Road. Fearing the worst, my parents have told my brother and me that we are all going out into the country that day and we are to have a picnic – something I have never come across before except in books. So, on this fateful Sunday morning what is occupying my mind is the imminent conjunction of life with literature; that I should remember nothing of the most

… Mr Chamberlain's broadcast finds us on a tram going down Tong Road.

momentous event in the twentieth century because of the prospect of an experience found in books was, I see now, a poor outlook for the future.

Nor is the lesson that life is never going to live up to literature slow in coming, since the much-longed-for picnic isn't eaten as picnics are in books, on a snowy tablecloth set in a meadow by a stream, but taken on a form in the bus station at Vicar Lane, where we wait half that day for any bus that will take us out of the supposedly doomed city.

Later that afternoon a bus comes, bound for Pateley Bridge, the other side of Harrogate. Some-where along the way and quite at random the four of us get off and our small odyssey is ended. It is a village called Wilsill, in Nidderdale. There are a few houses, a shop, a school and a church and, though we are miles from any town, even here the stream has been dammed to make a static water tank to serve the firefighters against the expected bombs. Opposite the bus-stop is a farm. My father is a shy man and, though I'm sure there are many larger acts of bravery being done elsewhere that day, to knock at the door of the farm and ask some unknown people to take us in still seems to me to be heroic. Their name is Weatherhead and they do take us in and without question, as people are being taken in all over England that first week of the war.

That night Dad takes the bus back to Leeds, my mother weeping as if he is returning to the front, and there at Wilsill we stay until, after a few weeks, it becomes plain nothing is going to happen for a while, and we go back to Leeds, leaving Byril Farm (which is now, alas, not a farm and has carriage lamps) standing out in my mind as the one episode in my childhood that lives up to the story-books.

Not yet at school when the war starts, I can already read, a precocious and I'm sure irritating child. Listening to grown-up conversation I see myself then as lost in a forest of names, particularly names that come out of the wireless, strange unspellable incantatory names that bear no relation to any that I have ever come across. There is Alvar Liddell, for instance, who often reads the news; no one I know is called Alvar, which in any case is pronounced Elvar and runs so smoothly off its namesake's tongue ('Here is the news and this is Alvar Liddell

Not yet at school when the war starts, I can already read, a precocious and I'm sure irritating child.

reading it') that I take it to be one name not two –
Elvarliddell, someone like Geraldo, say, or Mantovani,
so famous that his two names have melted into one as
tends to happen in the world of entertainment.

The war, of course, brings with it more strange
names. Some, like 'The Allies', I understand but what
or where is 'The Axis'? What is Vichy? I know it is
the bad side of the French and so I associate it with
vicious, though I also know it isn't quite as bad as
German and Nazi which, in retrospect, I suppose was
about right. But what is a quisling? Who is Laval?
They are among the regular cast featuring in news
bulletins but nobody ever seems to explain.

As hostilities move across Europe and the war
goes round the world, so the names change – Tobruk,
Benghazi, El Alamein – they are all of them faraway
places of which we know nothing. And it should have
been a kind of geography lesson, with schools urged
to keep a war map marked and up to date, though
none of the schools I attend 1939–45 can ever be
bothered.

It isn't just names that go unexplained. All
through the war there is a slogan painted on a wall in
Wellington Street: 'Start the Second Front now!' What
this means I never know at the time and it is still there

in the sixties when it falls, as most things eventually do in Leeds, to the bulldozer. When, with the invasion of Normandy in June 1944, the Second Front actually does start, I am still a bit confused. We are told at school that the invasion has begun and that this particular day is called D-day. I reason that if today is D-day there must logically already have been an A-day, a B-day and a C-day and that Leeds, as usual, being out of it and my family being out of it too, we have probably missed them. I note at the age of ten a fully developed ability not quite to enjoy myself, a capacity I have retained intact ever since.

Even the war turns out to be quite dull. There are no dog-fights in the mackerel skies over Armley, no mackerel skies much either, shrouded as Leeds generally is in smoke and grit. At night Dad dutifully patrols the Hallidays in his white ARP helmet, and the streets being dark and peaceful he then spends jolly evenings playing snooker in the wardens' post. No fires are started in Armley and unused after the first couple of years of the war is

Even the war turns out to be quite dull. There are no dog-fights in the mackerel skies over Armley …

the air-raid shelter outside our front door, unused that is except as a place to hide or to play, sometimes naughtily, so that builders' sand and unplastered brick I still associate, if not with sex, with the feelings that precede sex, feelings I know at the age of eight I should not be having and which no one else has but me.

The centre of Leeds is scarcely touched by the war, though coming through City Square in the summer of 1940 my mother sees soldiers who

... feelings I know at the age of eight I should not be having and which no one else has but me.

have been brought off at Dunkirk, laid out sleeping in full kit, dirty and unsmiling, the smell of them the same as the smell of soldiers she remembers from the First War and she comes home crying.

So deaths and dog-fights do not figure in my memories, my only recollection the drabness of things, a dullness intensified in ways lost to the memory. I had forgotten, for instance, what happened to the trams during the war, until one day in the sixties I chanced to see in the West End the exuberant million-aire Nubar Gulbenkian disembarking from his famous gold-plated taxi. The panels are decorated in a kind of wickerwork, which I take to be gold also, but what this recalls to me – and which I have entirely forgotten until this moment – is the adhesive yellow mesh that covers the wartime windows of the trams as a precaution against bomb blast and which, short of a small oval *oubliette*, prevents one from seeing out. The occasional loose end of this mesh is irresistible to picking fingers, so the advancing tide of the Allies across Europe corresponds with the receding tide of the mesh across the windows, stripped off entirely unofficially by passengers more and more confident of victory. So by 1945 we are back to clear glass again.

The drabness of my memories of the war and the sparseness of my memories altogether are a great discouragement to me when I begin to think about writing. What is there to write about? It was a childhood dull, without colour, my memories done up like the groceries of the time in plain, utility packets.

What is there to write about? It was a childhood dull without colour, my memories done up like the groceries of the time in plain, utility packets.

Films, it is true, injected memories so that
I might think I saw air-crews sitting out in armchairs
taking the sun on the edges of the runways at Dishforth
or Church Fenton, awaiting the signals for take-off.
But it is only films. Though I can remember passing a
newspaper hoarding and seeing that Leslie Howard is
dead, shot down over the Bay of Biscay...Leslie
Howard, a heart-throb of my mother's, the violin-
playing professor who defied the Gestapo in *Escape to
Happiness*, the Gestapo embodied, as it often is, in the
ample personage of Francis L. Sullivan, once seen,
wondrously, in Leeds walking down Thornton's
Arcade when presumably playing at one of the
theatres. It is Leslie Howard, too, who plays Mitchell,
the inventor of the Spitfire,
invented it in the nick of
time the film *First of the
Few* made out, the last
shot of him sitting in the
garden with a rug over
his knees (the rug a sure
sign he is dying) while
overhead, to the music of
William Walton, Spitfires turn and twist in the
summer skies.

... while overhead, to the music of William Walton, Spitfires turn and twist in the summer skies.

Our War

The war is a time of abeyance, an abatement
of ordinary life. For the Duration it is called, an end
to which to me as a child
is unimaginable. But, of
course, just as when the
war came nothing at first
happened, so when peace
comes and the Duration
ends, nothing happens

> *The war is a time
> of abeyance, an
> abatement of
> ordinary life.*

again – though this time not for six months but for
nearly six years – 1951 the first time one dares to think
that life might now be resumed.

War or no war, the wireless continues to turn
out a crop of names as memorable as they are unfath-
omable. A regular feature of *Children's Hour* is Toy
Town, written and adapted by S.G. Hulme Beaman,
the length and flavour of the name a necessary pro-
logue to the pleasures of Larry the Lamb and Ernest
the Policeman. Also on *Children's Hour* are Denis and
Mabel Constanduros. There is L. du Garde Peach, a
name that seems to exist purely as a name: I can't see
anyone being pointed out to me as L. du Garde Peach,
but this is partly because I wouldn't know what sex to
look for, the du Garde somehow masculine, the Peach
feminine, so the person unimaginable.

Years later when I came to read Proust, I found a great deal about names and their intrinsic flavour. The names that intrigued the young Marcel, though, were ancient names: Robert de Saint Loup en Bray, or the various names and titles of the Guermantes family, lichened in history and tradition. It was a far cry from Dino Galvani (of ITMA) or J. Mouland Begbie (leader of the BBC Scottish Orchestra) or that stalwart of the BBC Repertory Company and voice of Tammy Troot, Moultrie R. Kelsall. These are the names I remember. I had not yet begun to write at that time and so this falling short in the names department was another deterrent, a reminder that to write one had to have something to write out of, and my names like my memories didn't come up to scratch.

An Ideal Home

IT IS A CAUSE OF PAIN TO ME AS A BOY that the house we move to in Headingley in 1946 has no hallway and that you step from the outside directly into the kitchen-cum-living room.

This absence of a hallway and indeed of a front room isn't evidence of poverty particularly; it's simply that, with my father being a butcher, we live over the shop, and there's a shortage of rooms. It has other drawbacks, too. Fetching a bucket of coal, for instance, means going through the darkened cellar and edging past beast heads hanging from the ceiling, trying not to look at the cows' dead eyes and dodging the blood drizzling from their noses.

But most distasteful to me of all is Dad's insistence on rendering dripping in the cellar so that periodically the whole house reeks with the terrible smell of melting fat.

Were our house more shabby, it would sort better with the dripping, boiling and spitting down below. But my mother has transformed her ordinary little kitchen into a crude version of rooms she has seen pictured in tasteful magazines like *Ideal Home*. She's fixed a pelmet of flowered cretonne across the top of the black-leaded kitchen range, hung some horse brasses up one side and put her two battered

Staffordshire dogs in the hearth. On the ex-gramophone cabinet, bought when they were first married, is a green glass doorstop and a lustre cup and saucer. There is a Staffordshire greyhound without its tail, a sheep minus an ear, and all bathed in the soft light from a battered majolica vase Mam has turned into a lampholder. It's a nice cosy room and I am deeply ashamed of it, and never more so than when the stench of fat drifts up from the cellar to cling to the gathered cretonne and mist the polished brass, my father's bloody smock hanging behind the door amid these battered emblems of gentility.

It's a nice cosy room and I am deeply ashamed of it, and never more so than when the stench of fat drifts up from the cellar ...

Mam's agglomeration of bric-a-brac had begun back in 1943 with a workbox, though it isn't strictly speaking a workbox at all but an early nineteenth-century tea-caddy. She had spotted it in the dustbin of my father's wholly unlamented stepmother, thrown out after her death. Mam salvaged it and I have it still, used as it always has been as a workbox for needles and cotton. Seeing this coved walnut-veneered box on my own dresser, sixty years after she rescued it from the bin, I still find it shocking to think that anyone could ever have thought to throw it out.

But that my mother should have thought so at a time when such objects were not much sought after means, I suppose, that she already detects something in herself that is not in tune with her surroundings, and which in a sillier or a more vain woman might lead her to put on airs, talk posh or even dye her hair. This is the path taken by her sisters, their painful assaults on gentility a family joke. With my mother, though, it produces a kind of yearning so vague and unfocused it never stands a chance of fulfilment.

At one stage it leads to a frenzy for making lampshades, and these pink satin creations, generally with a hanging fringe, eventually come to feature in every room in the house. Another time it is crochet, when there is no ornament but acquires its own mat. But the most enduring of her hobbies – long before television makes it fashionable – is antiques or 'old things', as she calls them, not sure that to declare a liking for antiques isn't in itself pretentious.

So after the tea-caddy other items accumulate; there are Staffordshire figures which in those days are

still cheap and relatively easy to come by, though of the two dozen or so figures Mam acquires over the years only one is perfect, all the others maimed or in some way disfigured; they have lost arms or hands and the parrot that perches on the shoulder of an androgynous highlander in a kilt lacks its head. Sitting at the kitchen table on an evening, Mam fashions her version of a missing tambourine out of plasticine or makes a brave stab at a head of a sheep and glues crude prostheses to one-armed drummer boys – additions, particularly since she seldom gets round to painting them, that deceive no one and in time become almost as antique as the figures they are meant to renovate.

The mingling of these ceramic casualties with the stench of hot fat, though it shames me, does not surprise. It is just another example of how our family never manages to be like other families. My mother, for example, is convinced that every family in the country except us sits down to a cooked breakfast much as they do in her magazines. Even as a boy, I know this is nonsense, while at the same time managing myself to entertain assumptions even more foolish.

There is in our house, for instance, as I imagine there is in most houses lived in by couples who have gone through a wedding ceremony and the orgy of not always well-chosen present-giving that accompanies it, a quantity of crockery, table-linen and general household – *materiel* would be the word – that is surplus to requirements – table-napkins that are seldom used, tray cloths similarly; an embarrassment of cake- knives and even cake-forks. Here are a set of coffee spoons for the coffee we never drink; sugar tongs for the sugar lumps we never use, and a cheese knife that remains a stranger to cheddar.

Instead of regarding these items as a household's inevitable redundancies, as a boy I see all these disparate and unused utensils as evidence of failure. The fish slice, still pristine in its original box, is, it seems to me, a relic of a way of life we have not managed to keep up

Here are a set of coffee spoons for the coffee we never drink; sugar tongs for the sugar lumps we never use.

just as Dad has not kept up his fretwork or Mam her rug-making. Social standards must have slipped else why is the cake stand never put on the table or the serviette rings either? All these accumulated and outmoded objects seem to me as a child an indictment of us as family, a dossier of our social unsuccess. In a truly ideal home there would be fish for high tea served slice by slice at places with side- plates, each with its own napkin. If there is jam, it will be out of the chromium jampot holder, the spoon with the arms of Southport. There will be a slice for the cake, too, the crumbs swept up afterwards with a tray and brush like they have in the better class of boarding-house. Tea once cleared, there will be fretwork again for Dad and rug-making for Mam, and gathered round the table we will look like a family pictured on the cover of *John Bull* or featured in the tales of Enid Blyton.

This proper way of going on, I see as extending to the bedroom too, with my mother in front of the dressing-table mirror brushing her hair with the silver-backed brush that always lies there, dusty and unused, even powdering her face with the ancient powder puff that occupies one of the cut-glass vessels provided for the purpose, all components of the dressing-table set with which marriage has endowed her. She might even take off her rings and place them on the dish with a glass prong that is another of the dressing-table's unused features but which always mystifies me as a child. This is partly because my mother has no rings other than her wedding ring, which she never takes off, but it is also confused in my mind with another mysterious glass object in the kitchen cupboard, a fluted pyramid surrounded by a circle of glass teeth which I am told is used to make orange juice. Since this is during the war and there are no oranges, the process can never be demonstrated and so like the unused ring-prong it retains its mystery. Both objects turn up regularly now in village halls at sales of collectables.

... a fluted pyramid surrounded by a circle of glass teeth which I am told is to make orange juice.

As a child I root in the dressing-table drawers or squeeze the scrotum of the scent spray, cased in its tight silk net, thrusting it up my nose to catch a whiff of long dead 4711, scent in our house another thing that is just for show.

Years later I am going for the first time to France and ask Mam if there is anything I can bring her back.

'What's Chanel No.5?'

'Scent. Why?'

'There's often adverts for it. You could fetch me a bottle of that as a present. If it's too expensive you could get me Chanel No.4.'

So on that first visit to France I buy a little bottle, which she never actually uses but joins the other redundant accoutrements of the dressing-table, and is still there, forty years later, when she dies.

Every family has a secret and the secret is that it is not like other families. If only people knew what we were really like, my mother thought – her not getting up until ten in the morning and none of us sitting down to a proper breakfast – they'd have nothing to do with us. We pretend we're normal but it's only a matter of time before folks find out what we're like.

We pretend we're normal but it's only a matter of time before folks find out what we're like.

'Find out what?' I ask her grave.

Find out, I suppose, that Dad sleeps in his shirt and Mam in his old pyjama jacket, find out that most meals end with a piece of cake, find out that Mam keeps her teeth in a cup without a handle and Dad doesn't keep his in anything at all. Such creatures are not fit for polite society. Who could imagine such people? Who would want to know them?

In the sixth form one of my friends is a gentle, slightly older boy, John Totterdill, devout as I am and with whom I share an interest in architecture. He lives in West Park, one of the smarter suburbs of Leeds, the houses big and detached, his father, I think, a bank manager. One day John asks me back to tea. The sitting-room is vast and kitted out with all the uncomfortable appurtenances of middle-class living, including a nest of tables. Mrs Totterdill puts them out ready for our tea and, even though they are patently unsturdy, I take them to be stools rather than tables and so momentarily perch on one. A look of alarm crosses her face as she sees this lumpen boy bearing down on its delicate Edwardian legs and I instantly realise my mistake, then, of course, have to pretend that I have perched there only because I am so much at my ease, and pass off this *faux pas* as the product of a nonchalance I certainly do not feel. John Totterdill is dead, and his mother too, so the only person who remembers this incident is me and yet the embarrassment of it lives on.

My parents like John and he them, but with my misgivings about our living conditions, it is only on one occasion that he comes round to our house. Happily Dad isn't rendering dripping but I see to my shame that he has brought a pan to the table and left it there. I never ask John again. The depths of my triviality are discovered to me now fifty years later and there is no one left from whom to ask forgiveness.

A Shy Butcher

AS A CHILD I AM ALWAYS CONSCIOUS – and always guilty – that I love my mother more than my father. I am happier with her than with him, feel easier alone in her company, whereas with him I am awkward and over-talkative and not the kind of boy (modest, unassuming, unpretentious) that I feel he wants me to be and has been himself.

In my teens I become fearful that my mother and, to a lesser extent, my father will die. My concern is not entirely unselfish – 'What will happen to me?' probably at the bottom of it and it declares itself in an odd fashion.

Both my parents have false teeth. Dad has all his teeth out when he is twenty-five, and having been a martyr to toothache for much of his youth he counts himself well rid of them. With Mam it takes longer but eventually she has all hers out too. This is not unusual at the time, having your teeth out almost a rite of passage before entering middle age.

… having your teeth out almost a rite of passage before entering middle age.

So when I am fourteen or so, both my parents have long had false teeth (and called that, never dentures). At night Dad sleeps in his top set but takes out his bottom teeth and leaves them on the draining board. Mam, who is that much more hygienic, puts her set in a glass, or, more often, a cup that has lost its handle. They will have given them a perfunctory going-over with an ancient brush but the teeth are never immersed in any cleanser other than water so that they are always coated in a greyish lichen-like fur that is very hard to brush off, with Dad's teeth noticeably worse than Mam's as he is still in those days a smoker.

At fourteen I am convinced that this coating is a bad thing and that it harbours every known germ, and that my parents' health and indeed survival depends on it being removed. So, every night after they have gone to bed, I take it upon myself to scrub and swill their teeth to try and rid the plates of this grey accretion, noting even then that the proportion of dentures I have to do, two for Mam and one for Dad, corresponds fittingly with the respective degree of affection I bear, or think I bear, for each of them.

That I undertake this nightly ritual cleansing is never acknowledged by them or referred to by me, but it must seem odd, particularly to my father. What is this strange creature they have nurtured ... still at fourteen looking like a boy of ten, never away from

church or the library, and given to furtively scrubbing
their false teeth? It's no wonder that Dad seems to
have little time for me or that there are none of the
conventional rows he's had with my brother at the
same age and who is already asserting his indepen-
dence in the stock ways, smoking on the quiet, coming
home tipsy once or twice – stages in adolescence Dad
has long been led to expect. But who has ever heard of
a son who scrubs his parents' false teeth? The best
plan is to say nothing and hope that it will pass.

My father is a butcher, working until he's forty
for the Leeds Co-op and then branching out on his
own in a succession of small shops which make us a
living but not much more. He doesn't look like a
butcher, should never have been one, my mother says,
and would have been happier as a violinist.

His mother had been a rural schoolteacher, a
woman of great gentleness and strong character (and
who gave all the men in our family their big chin). She
dies when my father is five and, with a family of four
boys to bring up, it is not long before my grandfather
marries again. This time his choice is less fortunate, a
harsh and bitter woman, a stalwart of the chapel who
makes the boys' lives a misery. She tells lies to my
grandfather about his sons, so that having beaten them

herself, when he comes home from work he beats them again. Starving them so that they often have to be fed by neighbours, she is a stepmother out of the fairy story.

What this woman's actual name is I don't know since whenever talk in the family turns to her she is always referred to as the Gimmer. This is probably a nickname bestowed on her by my father as he is always good at mythologising people, and being a butcher would know what a gimmer is – a sheep that has had no lambs. It is the Gimmer who had put him to butchery in the first place, at the age of twelve, and I suspect that this is the continuing offence for which he cannot forgive her, for never was there a more unsuitable butcher.

What possesses my father to want to teach himself the violin I cannot think, as it must be one of the most discouraging instruments for a beginner, nor is there encouragement at home, where he is made to practise in the freezing parlour, the only light what comes in from the street lamp through the window.

It's a scene that would seem melodramatic in Dickens. But somehow he learns to play and to play well. He has what I take to be perfect pitch and can pick up his violin and play along with the wireless, sometimes saying the notes as he plays. I see him now on a Sunday night, hearkening to the sound of his fiddle and playing along to Albert Sandler and the Palm Court Orchestra and follow it up with the hymns on *Sunday Half Hour*. But he is modest about his accomplishments and in ways that I don't notice, so that it's only when I am looking for photographs for this programme that I realise there are none of him with his violin.

Central to my mother and father's way of looking at things is the conviction that they aren't quite like other people. This extends to clothes. Dad wears a suit every day of his life – not a smart suit, just a working suit, though always with a waistcoat. He has this suit and what he calls 'My Other Suit', which he keeps for best. Except that one is more worn than the other, they are identical and when the working suit gets too worn the Other Suit is demoted to be the working suit, and he buys a replacement, exactly the same, for best.

When he retires, both he and my mother make an

effort to live up to what they feel their lives ought to be and this includes clothes. Briefly, Mam gets him to what she calls 'branch out' and change his style. So once, arriving at Lancaster Station where they are to meet me, I am shocked to find my mother waiting with what I take to be another man. But it is only my father dressed in what I suppose must be described as Leisurewear – a check sports coat, a two-tone cardigan, soft-collared shirt and Hush Puppies, the name of which Mam cannot remember and so calls them push buttons. To my relief, this sartorial revolution is short-lived and not to Dad's taste, and it's not long before the new outfit is relegated to clothes for doing the garden and he goes back to the old regime of 'My Suit' and 'My Other Suit'.

To my relief, this sartorial revolution is short-lived and not to Dad's taste …

The war between the sexes is not a campaign in which Dad ever enlists. When he retires, my mother, who is no more of a natural joiner than he is, nevertheless enrols in the Women's Institute. Now, if the WI ladies go off on a trip, Dad goes along too, wholly unconcerned that he is the only man in the party and, if only because he doesn't drink and seldom swears, he would probably have felt more uncomfortable were the opposite to be the case and he found himself in all male company.

He made you believe in Dickens and the unlikely goodness of some of his characters, as it is hard to see where his natural refinement had come from.

During the war he ekes out his butcher's pay by getting a fretsaw and making wooden toys to patterns from *Hobbies* magazine. These he hawks round Leeds without much success, until he finds quite a posh toy shop down County Arcade that will take all he can make, though at a reduced price. His speciality is penguins which he puts on a four-wheeled cart that a child can pull. These penguins he cuts out in front of the fire, sitting pedalling the fretsaw (a paper down against the sawdust) on the hearthrug at Halliday Place. Then he marks up their contours and paints them in the scullery where they are ranged on top of the wringer to await the finishing touch, the eye. I see these ranks of sightless birds standing there blank then, suddenly, with a touch of his paint brush acquiring character.

My parents are always everything to each other and my clearest memory of the war is of Mam's tearful leave-takings from my father, often on

Harrogate Bus Station, though there is something ridiculous about them as he is going back – not to certain death, but only to Leeds and Armley Lodge Co-op. Or it might be at Morecambe, where my brother and I walk with my mother across the hard-ribbed sands up at the West End when, having put him on the train, she is still weeping bitterly and, though the parting is only for four or five days, it's every bit as tragic as if he is bound for the Middle East.

... my clearest memory of the war is of Mam's tearful leave-takings of my father.

My second television play, *Sunset Across the Bay*, is set in Morecambe, and has a farewell scene on those same sands which is every bit as sad. I write it with no premonitions but when a few months later it virtually comes to pass, I wished I hadn't. Anyone who writes is aware that the act of writing carries with it a degree of involuntary prediction, the future, as it were, let out of the bag. So it's on the same sands that I have staged a fictional farewell that, a few months later, Mam and Dad take their last walk together. Unknown to her, and perhaps unknown to him, his heart is giving out. She walks ahead across the sand, looking at the sunset, only he has stopped.

'Nay, Mam,' he says 'I'm jiggered. We shall have to go back.'

There are no tears now, when the occasion genuinely warrants it, as neither of them realises the seriousness of what is happening. But ten days later he is dead.

A few weeks after he dies, I go to Scotland to stay with friends by a remote loch in Morven. It is early evening when I arrive and they are out for the day so I sit outside the cottage in the last of the sunshine and make some notes about my father.

He always washed up.

He generally liked to be in bed before my mother and slept on the right.

He always wore black shoes.

He often picked up stuff in the street – coins, naturally, but which pleased him out of all proportion to their value; nuts, screws, bits that had fallen off cars. Mam disapproved of this habit lest the things might be dirty.

He has no smell at all, and when he dies scarcely a grey hair; paleish blue eyes and a worn red face brimming over with kindness and pleasure. When he

washed, he dried his face so vigorously that it
squeaked.

Now the holiday party has returned and I put
away these notes. Joan says that two miners from
Falkirk have come to camp by the loch. They sleep
all day and fish all night and every morning she
finds a cleaned and gutted sea-trout waiting on the
window sill.

Days Out

TELL SOMEONE THAT YOU LIVE or have lived in Leeds
and they are quite likely to say, 'Well, it's easy to get
out of,' and this is true, the roads to freedom being
north to the Dales or east to the Vale of York.

When I was a child, though, escape wasn't at all
easy, Leeds quite hard to get out of in wartime,
particularly on a Sunday which was my father's only
day off. Though trams run to the outskirts of the city
and beyond – to Guiseley, for instance, on the edge of
Ilkley Moor, or to Lawnswood, only a mile or two
from Wharfedale – to go off by tram, in my childish
view, doesn't constitute a proper day out; we go by
tram every day of the week, after all. A proper day
out means going by bus except that on a Sunday with
petrol being restricted the buses don't start until
midday and are always full.

So Sunday mornings in the early forties generally
find my mother and father, my brother and me queuing
in one of two places: outside the YWCA in Cookridge
Street (now the Henry Moore Study Centre) or on
King Street, just down from the Metropole Hotel and
opposite the Caressa hosiery and underwear building,
the dancing exponent of which in silk stockings and
slip disports herself on the front of the works in the
form of a neon sign (never, of course, in those days

lit), her gay abandon a reminder, as I see it, of how carefree life must have been in the days before the war.

Which bus we choose to queue for, in one sense, makes no difference. My childhood has little in common with that of Proust except that both routes resemble his fictional Guermantes and Combray in this (and only in this) that each in the end brings you to the same place, namely Wharfedale: King Street the start of the Guiseley Way, Cookridge Street if we want to go via Lawnswood.

There will be already a sizeable queue at the bus stop, mostly hikers like ourselves. Except that they aren't like us; or we aren't like them. They are in shorts, most likely, and various sorts of outdoor gear, the women in ankle socks and berets, probably, with very much in vogue waterproof windjammers (which are not yet called anoraks) and generally beige, colour being something that is on hold for the Duration.

Conformist that I am at seven years old, nothing would make me happier than to be garbed thus and so like everybody else. Instead Dad is in his Other Suit, i.e. the suit he doesn't wear to work, waistcoat included, with his trilby hat and raincoat over his arm, in the pockets of which are the flask and our sandwiches. Mam is in hat and coat, too, wearing her ordinary shoes and clutching her inevitable handbag; she might just as well be going shopping at Matthias Robinson's as hiking on the moors. Gordon and me are in our gabardine raincoats, school caps with collar and tie, short trousers and long grey stockings and shoes – an outfit (largely from Rawcliffe's on Boar Lane) that these days would stamp us as children of the middle class, but which then is the normal garb of every schoolboy, though not when they are going off hiking for the day.

Our get-up makes no concessions to the activity at all, so that to see us waiting in that queue on Cookridge Street we might have been off to church or to visit a grave, certainly not bound for a picnic. As we get off the bus at Burley in Wharfedale we look less like hikers than those refugees who, a year or two earlier, were being dive-bombed by Stukas and plunging into ditches along the roads of northern France.

… we might have been off to church or to visit a grave, certainly not bound for a picnic.

Getting off at our stop may well be our first glimpse of the countryside as standing downstairs in the always crowded bus one sees nothing and even

upstairs is as bad as many of the Ledgard buses have
an aisle on the right and a long six seater on the left: a
child stuck in the middle of one of these and wreathed
as upstairs always is in cigarette smoke, can see nothing
of the world outside.

So when Dad makes the special little kissing noise
which he uses to call cats and cows and reassemble his
scattered family, it marks the end of an ordeal that is
often slightly sick-making and we stumble thankfully
down the stairs into the fresh air of Wharfedale.
Hearing that mock kiss now, nearly sixty years later,
I would get to my feet knowing this is our stop.

Hiking is most memorable in the autumn when
we pick blackberries, or 'blegs' as Dad calls them, but
even on these modest expeditions we still manage not
to toe what I see as the standard line. The routine
receptacle for blackberries carried by practically all
the other pickers is a blue and silver government-issue
Dried Milk tin. Dried Milk doesn't figure in our diet
so neither does the tin, and the Bennett's blackberries
are gathered in blue Tate and Lyle sugar bags, which,
though handier, invariably get soggy with the blackberry juice and if you're not careful suddenly give
way, scattering their painfully harvested contents all
over the ground, and (if seen by Mam) not to be

picked up as this renders them polluted and therefore unusable. Sometimes it's bilberries we pick, but we never see, still less gather, mushrooms; we never see a heron, a not uncommon bird; I never recall a hawk, a fox or even a hedgehog. It's as if nature is in short supply along with everything else in the forties and that, too, has been put on hold for the Duration.

In fact, only three times do I remember wild life impinging. Once when we're bilberrying on the moors above Shipley there is a plague of tiny frogs, swarming in thousands out of the rust-coloured streams and jumping all over the heather. Having raised innumerable tadpoles, all of which expired long before they had got to the frog stage, my brother and I find this plague of frogs almost miraculous. But we have nothing in which to carry any of them home, apart, that is, from the empty vacuum flask and, Mam being as fastidious as she is, there is no hope of using that. We take a few home in a paper bag but they are unsurprisingly dead on arrival.

On another occasion, crossing some fields near Otley, in one of the streams we see a crayfish. And one morning in Nidderdale, climbing up a narrow lane above Wilsill by a spring of clear water, I see a lizard on a rock. And that's it so far as nature in my child-

hood is concerned ... a few frogs, a crayfish and a lizard. When I think of all the Sundays we went off hiking it seems a meagre harvest and at the time it confirms me in my suspicion that with nature, as in other departments, adults pretended. It was a conspiracy, and books, the wall charts in the classroom, the Romany programmes on *Children's Hour* are all in on it, all concerned to conceal the fact that nature is dull.

The wall chart has a picture of a kingfisher. I know I am never going to see a kingfisher in Armley, but with the environs of Leeds scoured by hikers every Sunday even in Wharfedale the chances are pretty slim. Besides, as one of my schoolfellows said, 'Anyway, all birds are brown.'

And the seaside is the same. The charts in the classroom show monster shells, star-fish and even seahorses. Well, not in my experience and certainly not at Morecambe. But it is a conspiracy in which we schoolchildren collaborate. The class paints pictures of the seaside, but none of us paints the sea brown or the sand grey, though that's how they are at Morecambe. Nor do we paint the barbed wire or the tank traps that litter the sands. No, we paint

… none of us paints the sea brown or the sand grey …

the sea blue and the sand yellow and the sun always shining, like it does in the books and in that pre-war Eden we cannot remember.

Once only does nature live up to the publicity, life and art coincide, and it's at the farmhouse in Nidderdale to which we are briefly evacuated. There, life is like the storybooks with an old horse we can ride, a sow with her piglets, calves we feed out of a bucket and eggs to be collected from the grass where the silly hens have laid them.

It is there on a Thursday morning I see the lizard and I know it's a Thursday because we're on our way to Ripon Market. And when we go on to wait for the bus at the lane end there are soldiers camped in a field and a couple of them, half naked, are scraping their plates and swilling out their billy cans just over the wall. They joke with my brother and me as a way of flirting with Mam, who is laughing and confused, and remembering it years afterwards I see that she must have been not only loving and nice, which I knew, but also pretty.

Dogged, dutiful, repetitious these hiking trips seem to me as a child, the only excitement there is being to do with bulls. As a butcher, Dad is in what's called a reserved occupation and is immune from the call-up. Slaughtermen have no such immunity, unsurprisingly in view of their trade – but this means that the butchers have themselves to do a stint at the slaughter-house which is below Kirkgate Market. My father is a gentle man, not cut out to be a butcher, still less a slaughterman, and he finds these sessions a great trial. They leave him with a lifelong hatred of the cruelty involved, particularly that to do with ritual slaughter which he thinks is barbarous; it's the only subject on which he ever writes letters to the papers.

My father is a gentle man, not cut out to be a butcher, still less a slaughterman ...

What these sessions also do is instil in Dad a healthy respect for bulls which, given the conditions in the slaughterhouse, regularly run amok. So when we are out hiking and come across a bull he insists on our taking what seem absurd precautions. Not merely will he not let us cross the field with the bull in it, which is understandable, but even when we are on the other side of a substantial wall he insists on the family scuttling by bent double as if we are on manoeuvres.

This fear of bulls never leaves him though, given the right circumstances, he can be bolder. It is quite late in life that he learns to drive and now, spotting a bull in a field, there is no cringing behind a wall. Instead he stops and, safe in the Mini, winds down the window and shouts at the blameless quadruped, 'Gerron, you bad sod!' and then puts his foot down and scoots away.

Liberation for my parents has been a long time coming, as it's not until he's sixty-five and against all expectations, particularly his own, that my father passes his driving test. Now for the first time in their lives my parents stop feeling different, Dad's final achievement

Now for the first time in their lives my parents stop feeling different ...

to show that he can, if he really puts his mind to it, be just the same as anybody else.

The few years they have left together are a kind of heyday, Dad happy in his new-found skill, Mam no longer constrained to speak in the undertone she always adopts on the bus but free in the isolation of the car to comment on the passing scene:

'I thought that was a feller in a raincoat bending down, only it's two sheep.'

'I wouldn't want to be as bald as he is. You'd never know where to stop washing your face.' And once, when a bearded driver threatens to pull out in front of them: 'Get back, Tolstoy.'

And they would both be laughing, still silly and full of fun and driving towards the dark.

Proper Names

My parents' names are Lilian and Walter, Lil and Walt as they call each other. Except that they don't very often, particularly after my brother and I are born, which somehow puts paid to their names. When we come along, Walter and Lilian are buried and there-after they are almost always called Mam and Dad, not merely by us, but by each other, their names deferring to their function as parents.

... Walter and Lilian are buried and thereafter they are almost always called Mam and Dad ...

Occasionally, though, function forgotten, they resume their identities and become people again and it is always at times of pain or stress. As when, some-time in the early forties, Mam has the last of her teeth out. Dad has had all of his taken out at one go when he is twenty-five, but Mam loses hers more slowly, until one of her front teeth having decayed so spectac-ularly it looks as if it may snap off, she has all of hers out too.

After this wholesale extraction she is in terrible pain. Someone tells her that cigarettes help and we come home from school to find her crouched over the fire inexpertly puffing at one of Dad's cigs (the first and only time in her life that she smokes), her legs, as women's were in those days, mottled red and black from sitting too close to the fire. When Dad comes home, he isn't Dad but Walt and she is Lil, holding his hand and weeping by the fire with a vinegar and brown paper plaster stuck to her aching face.

The next time Mam is Lil is just after the war when Dad, who is unemployed and has been ill on and off for six months, collapses one Sunday morning in the street in Armley and, having managed to reach the house of a friend, he lies on the floor crying out with excruciating pain.

He is a patient of Dr Moneys who has hitherto dismissed his symptoms as 'wind', prescribing what Dad calls 'another bottle of that chalky muck' and which my brother or I are sent down the road to fetch from Timothy White's the chemists. The chalky muck doesn't do the trick and whatever it is that has felled Dad to the kitchen floor, it plainly isn't wind.

The chalky muck doesn't do the trick and whatever it is that has felled Dad to the kitchen floor, it plainly isn't wind.

Dramatic though the circumstances are, a doctor is not lightly to be called out on a Sunday morning, though how readily a doctor does 'come out', particularly at night or out of hours, is what makes him, irrespective of his diagnostic skills, a good doctor, and certainly a good doctor to be with – 'He'll always come out,' the highest praise a patient can bestow.

This is 1946, on the eve of the introduction of the National Health Service, and the Armley doctors Dr Gordon and Dr Dalrymple are still rather lofty figures, living in some style, or in detached houses anyway with brass plates on the gateposts, and on this Sunday morning probably up at Adel playing golf.

Even in poorer Wortley where we are currently living with Grandma, the doctors are quite grand, Dr Moneys and Dr Slaney, distinguished silver-haired figures exercising a paternal sway over their slum practices, not poor particularly or seem-ingly over-worked, and still with all the old-fashioned accoutrements of their profession – the pin-stripe suit, the watch chain and the Humber

… distinguished silver-haired figures exercising a paternal sway over their slum practices …

parked in the empty street – so that any visit by the doctor is noted by neighbours in those otherwise carless days.

But before it's decided to get a doctor or an ambulance, someone runs up the street to knock on the door of a woman who knows a bit about medicine and minor ailments to see if she can gauge the urgency of the situation. Someone else must have run up to the Whingate terminus to get a tram down to Wortley to fetch my mother, whose name Dad is now calling, and that it is 'Lil' he is calling, not 'Mam', diagnosis enough that whatever the woman up the street may say, he, at least, thinks he is dying.

That there is a wise woman on hand is not unusual, as such figures are a customary part of working-class life and provide an unofficial auxiliary medical service. In those days, though, the remedies they purveyed and their dabbling in matters medical at all were more officially disparaged, any resort to them to be kept quiet when seeing 'the proper doctor'.

There is no shortage of such folk doctors. The street in which Dad has collapsed is in the Moorfields, and this group of streets is home to such a woman. We had once lived half a mile away in the Hallidays and there is one there too, a Miss Thompson. She is

someone to whom Dad goes with minor complaints
and generally boils, a boil particularly on the back of
the neck a more regular affliction than it is now, the
square of lint and the sticking plaster with which it is
covered making the sufferer walk in a way both stiff-
necked and wary, thus imparting to their gait a
vaguely Vorticist slant. Miss Thompson generally
blames the blood and prescribes burdock root, which
is bought at a herbalist in one of the back streets near
Leeds Market where herbs jostle with trusses and
remedies for piles and
more complicated and
mysterious surgical
appliances that make it a
shaming place for a child
to visit – or a child like
me, anyway.

*... Leeds market
where herbs jostle
with trusses and
remedies for piles ...*

Originating in such a marginal emporium the
burdock, at any rate in my mother's eyes, retains a
taint of the truss and so has to be prepared in a strictly
circumscribed fashion, steeped in a special basin
before being boiled up in a chipped blue enamel pan,
uniquely designated for the purpose as 'the herb pan',
and never to be used for the sprouts, say, or the
potatoes; Dad dosing himself with the resultant liquid

over a longish period generally without bothering to decant it from the pan, a practice my mother predictably deplores.

Besides the blood, wise women like Miss Thompson are apt understandably to lay the blame for the body's ailments on the bowels, so when today the wise woman comes down the street, still wiping her hands on her apron from doing the Sunday dinner, she takes one look at Dad and blames constipation and for this she has the remedy to hand. Dr Moneys, at his most airily detached, could not have got it more wrong or embarked on a procedure more calculated to give excruciating pain and broadcast the infection throughout the gut, because what Dad is suffering from, screaming out with now, is a perforated ulcer and what she is suggesting is an enema.

... she takes one look at Dad and blames constipation and for this she has the remedy to hand.

Perhaps she brings her own enema, though in any case there would be one in the house, as there certainly is in ours.

Coiled black and serpentine in its almost new box, with the instructions pasted underneath the lid, the enema looks like a section of the innards it is meant to irrigate, the hard liquorice-coloured bulb at the same time suggesting some ancient musical instrument. I feel it must have been precaution more than necessity because ours has never been used; otherwise no amount of washing would manage to cleanse it, and it would certainly not be in the sideboard drawer as, in Mam's eyes, use would have polluted it for all eternity and it would have been consigned to the murky cupboard below the bathroom basin or stowed with other per-manently tainted articles in the ghetto behind the cistern.

… it would have been consigned to the murky cupboard below the bathroom basin or stowed with other permanently tainted articles in the ghetto behind the cistern.

By the time my brother and I arrive in our caps and gabardine raincoats, never other than neat even in the presence of death – or what we think is death – it is to find Dad, his torture just having been administered, laid out on the floor of this strange kitchen, with Mam holding his hand as he gives

vent to the terrible cries of her name.

'Lil.' 'Lil.' 'Lil.' And it is the name as much as anything that tells us this must be death.

Now the ambulance arrives and he is taken to St James's – these days known nationwide as Jimmy's from its numerous TV appearances. It isn't then – St James's just a poor alternative to the Infirmary. Both, though, are old hospitals, Gothic and even picturesque, and it's in one of the wards, now I think a museum, where Dad is admitted to be operated on that night, my brother and I kneeling down by our attic beds to pray for him like children in a Victorian painting.

For almost a week he is critical and nowadays would, I suppose, have been kept in Intensive Care. Each patient has a number, printed every night in the *Yorkshire Evening Post*, Dad's often in the dreaded category, 'Friends may visit', the words unprinted being 'before it's too late'. He catches pneumonia, as patients tend to do, and for a time is moved into the bed by the door, the significance of which I only learn years later at the Old Vic when watching Peter Nichols' play *The National Health*, the bed by the door generally taken to be the anteroom to the mortuary.

... he catches pneumonia as patents tend to do and for a time is moved into the bed by the door ...

But it isn't, and eventually Dad pulls round, is brought home to Grandma's at Gilpin Place where a bed is made up in the sitting room, and he lies in state, waiting eagerly for my brother and me to come home from school every afternoon when he can ask us what we've been doing, something that he has never done before, maybe because he hasn't had the opportunity, but which makes me think, almost for the first time, that perhaps he actually likes me.

But now things are back to normal, Lil and Walt banished again; he is Dad and she is Mam, their names put back in the drawer to be kept for best – or worst. Or perhaps, too, for those times when I wake in the night and hear them in bed, talking and laughing, being themselves.

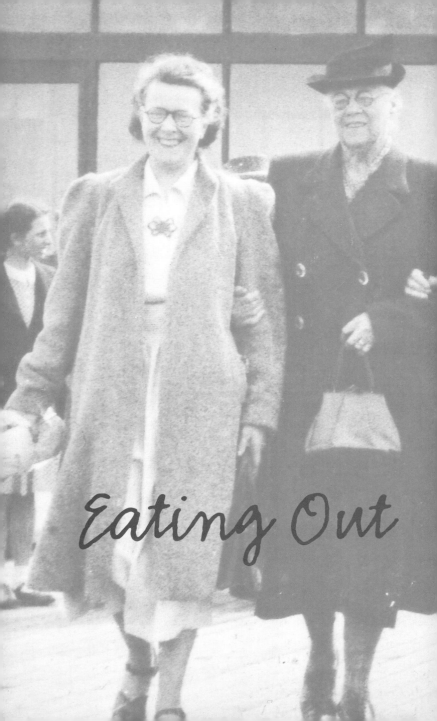

Eating Out

'SALAD'S ON A NEW FOOTING NOW, APPARENTLY,' Mam said, looking at her copy of *Ideal Home*. 'It doesn't just have to be lettuce and tomato and a slice of boiled egg. They eat celery with apple now and you can put raisins in if you want. All the boundaries are coming down.'

This would, I suppose, be in the fifties, datable in my own experience from my first encounter, at some Oxford party I thought sophisticated, with pineapple chunks spiked with cheese on a stick, where I ate the pineapple and smuggled the cheese into my handkerchief. The tide of sophistication reaches Leeds a bit later, when we have similar problems but in a café.

'Be careful, Dad,' said Mam. 'There's walnuts in this salad. They won't do for you. Leave them on the edge of your plate then I'll put them in the serviette.'

'Why can't he just not eat them?' I ask irritated, I suppose, because I recognise my own timidity in hers.

'Because it's not fair on them,' said Mam. 'They don't want disheartening. If they're making an effort to branch out a bit we don't want to put the tin hat on it.'

'Did you like your salad?' asks the waitress.

'Yes. It was very unusual,' Mam said. 'Though we're not used to raisins in savoury things. Of course that's all the rage now, isn't it?'

Eating Out

Nor does it stop at salads. Mam is on the telephone. 'Your Dad and me went in one of these Expresso places today and I had some of this coffee with all the foam on top. Have you tried it? The machine makes a right din. And it's a dear do because once you're through all the froth and that, there's only half a cup. Your Dad had tea, of course. Mind you, we both had glass cups.'

They are regulars at the café in Schofield's department store in the Headrow, which they had patronised certainly since the war when it was one of the few establishments still managing to serve cakes with a species of cream. With its hushed elegance and soft lighting it is socially on a par with Matthias Robinson's in Briggate, both of them spacious and thickly carpeted emporiums, at any rate on the ground floor, which invariably sell jewellery, perfume and haberdashery with the café always at the top.

Schofield's café is notable for a suave *maître d'* (not that we would have called him that then or indeed known what to call him). As a child I think him so grand he probably owns the store. With thick brown hair brushed back from his forehead and a thin moustache, he looks not unlike the then popular film star George Brent. What is most notable about him, though, is that on one of his hands, or what I think of as one of his hands, he wears a black leather glove. I do not as a child associate this with disability, taking the glove rather as a part of his professional equipment. It is, after all, on the hand with which he generally shows you to your table, so I assume, without ever reasoning it out, that it is gloved because it gets more wear than the other hand. Unruffled and always with a half smile, he is often the only man in a café full of women and bestows on this provincial establishment an air of immense sophistication so that following him and the gloved hand to a table I feel, as so often in cafés, that we are there on false pretences and shortly to be found out.

This dread of imminent exposure is more acute if we ever venture up the social scale and have tea in Marshall and Snelgrove's in Park Row (the site now squatted by the uninspiring bulk of Lloyd's Bank). Marshall and Snelgrove's is a provincial

... This dread of imminent exposure is more acute if we ever venture up the social scale and have tea in Marshall and Snelgrove's ...

Eating Out

outpost of a store in London's West End, so has a
certain metropolitan grandeur, the carpets thicker,
voices more hushed and fur coats much in evidence,
and though the menu caters to Mam's core requirement
of tea and toasted tea-cakes, tea-cakes come under an
EPNS dishcover, the proper manipulation of which is
an additional hazard to the terrors of eating out.

Heightened respectability brings other perils
too as, lacking a pianist or a string trio, the café at
Marshall and Snelgrove's lays on a floor show. As
Mam tries to catch the waitress's eye in order to get
some more hot water ('We like it weak, you see'), she
intercepts instead the far less sympathetic glance of
one of the resident mannequins who prowl the aisles
between the tables modelling outfits on offer on the
floor below in the couture department. Released
from the confines of the cat-walk, these tall elegant
creatures with their neat heads (the forties film star
Greta Gynt comes to mind) take on an almost preda-
tory air, gliding between the tables on the look-out for
victims. Picking out a table, the model executes a tight
pirouette to swing wide her 'New Look' skirt,
allowing her in the process to slip off her bolero
jacket which, looped over her finger, she slings
casually over one shoulder before sauntering back.

Schooled by auction sales at Hepper and Sons Mam keeps her eyes down, lest meeting the glance of one of these disdainful creatures might mark her out as a potential purchaser, on the off-chance I suppose that she might be considering exchanging what she calls 'my little swagger coat with the green buttons I got in Richard Shops', for a shawl-collared dirndl-skirted number in green shantung with detachable panels and matching jacket. Not that the model is likely to waste much time on a dumpy middle-aged woman with a thirteen-year-old son in a gabardine raincoat bent on making a toasted tea-cake go a long way. There is no point in demonstrating for them how a conventional Jaeger two-piece for casual daytime wear can, by dint of undoing one or two gold blazer buttons and reversing the jacket, be transformed into an altogether more exciting ensemble suitable for the evening – a cocktail dress, in fact.

Not that the model is likely to waste much time on a dumpy middle-aged woman with a thirteen year-old-son in a garbardine raincoat ...

My mother has never had a cocktail dress for the simple reason that she has never had a cocktail. This does not stop her finding the world of cocktail parties mysterious and exciting. Schooled on what she reads in *Woman's Own*, she is always convinced that a round of coffee mornings and cocktail evenings is how other women spend their time, and that she doesn't is yet another of the shortcomings that mark the Bennett family off from the rest of the human race. The glamour of cocktail parties partly resides in the mystery of the drinks that are on offer there. A cocktail she takes to be bright green, probably, with bobbing about in it a maraschino cherry the size of a fishing float.

And it isn't merely the drink she misconceives, though with both she and my father being teetotallers it is understandable she should. The nearest they ever come to a drink is at Holy Communion and they utterly overestimate its effect. Dad learns to drive quite late in life, but however bad the weather they never drive to church for fear that the sacrament might make him incapable on the return journey.

But, as I say, it isn't just the drink at cocktail parties that my mother finds mysterious but the food that is on offer there too – cocktail snacks, sausages on sticks – food, I suppose, that nowadays would come under the generic term of nibbles. Now sausages are not uncommon in our house; my father is a butcher, after all, and we take them in our stride. But a sausage has only to be hoisted onto a stick to become for my mother an emblem of impossible sophistication.

But a sausage has only to be hoisted on a stick to become for my mother an emblem of impossible sophistication.

Of course, these days the stuff of what for Mam were dreams is readily available: dates, as the package says, enrobed in smoked salmon, brie and bacon parcels, sausages already cooked and kitted out with sticks, the essence of any smart gathering now on offer at Marks and Spencer ('A Leeds firm', as my aunties would always point out). Finger buffets, fork suppers, life with the crusts off – office party

fodder, I think of it – estate agents holding awkward
get-togethers with young couples in show-houses, a
farewell do in the photocopying room for Tanya,
who's off to Saudi and pastures new. The function of
functions has changed, and has, together with so
much that was socially exclusive, been diluted, come
downmarket, been made ordinary and everyday. Take
pot-pourri, for instance, which I first read of scenting
the red-lacquered rooms of Ottoline Morrell's house
at Garsington, or adding atmosphere to the painted
boiseries of Duncan Grant and Vanessa Bell at
Charleston, but which is nowadays the staple of every
garage. So perhaps the cocktail party and the notion
of gracious living that went with it was a general
aspiration, not peculiar
to my mother, a non-
party-going, non-party-
giving shy middle-aged
woman in the suburbs
of Leeds, who dreamed
of something different.
Perhaps there were
thousands like her,

*Perhaps there were
thousands like her,
aching as she did, for
something she could
not define ...*

aching as she did, for something she could not define
but who now see it all come to pass, made possible

via Marks and Spencer. Or, as Simon and Garfunkel sang (though not to my mother), 'All your dreams are on their way.'

As for cafés, though, I sometimes think of my mother and father now when I'm in one of those fancier restaurants where the meal kicks off with those tasty little appetisers the food fanatics are pleased to call an '*amuse-gueule*' – tiny quenelles of sole in a blackberry coulis, for instance, pheasant liver thrust inside a prune. It would have been risky for a restaurant to offer Mam and Dad anything of that nature as, far from being an appetiser, given a plate of bread and butter and a pot of tea to go with it, that would have been all they'd want or, as Mam might have said, 'We've had sufficient now, thank you.'

Whatever the food on offer and however much the complexion of cafés changed over the years, these little outings of my parents would always end in the same way with Dad standing in the inevitable raincoat and trilby holding my mother's handbag. Because once they have had their tea and paid the bill, invariably on the way out Mam stops to spend a penny, entrusting her handbag to my father with the injunction, always the same and never omitted: 'Dad, don't let anyone touch my bag.' This was in consequence of once there being no hook behind the lavatory door, so that she had had to put her bag on the floor.

Dad is left holding this shaming object, which he tries to smother with his raincoat, or holds it slightly away from him and not by the handle in order to proclaim that he and ladies' handbags are things apart.

Comic though it is, I see this ritual with the handbag now as one of the unquestioned accommodations my parents make to each other and which are as much evidence of love and affection as any of the conventional words my father, in particular, would have found it hard to utter.

Aunt Eveline

INSOFAR AS MY MOTHER EVER VOICES any ambitions for
my brother and me, it is that we should become
gentlemen farmers earning £10 a week. This would
have been in the early forties when £500 a year is a
not unrespectable income, though why she has settled
on farming, gentlemanly or otherwise, and for which
neither of us have any inclination – is not plain.
Getting away from Leeds has something to do with it,
probably, escape always attractive to my mother,
particularly an escape from the north – or the dark,
satanic mills aspect of it anyway.

It is this, I think, that makes her very occasionally
urge on me the attractions of the writer's life, instanc-
ing the novels of Leo Walmsley or Naomi Jacob –
even, going up the scale a bit, the Brontë sisters,
whom she has never actually read, but thinks of as
local girls who have kicked over the traces and made
good Down South. The novelist and ex-Bingley
librarian John Braine of *Room at the Top* fame will
later come into the same category.

The only writer she does read with any regularity,
though, has nothing to do with the north at all. This is
Beverley Nichols, of whose column in *Woman's Own*
she is a devoted fan, and whose life, Beverley writing
about his gardens and chronicling the doings of his

several cats, seems to my mother one of dizzying sophistication. I don't share this admiration nor the literary ambition she occasionally wishes upon me. Had I had any thoughts of 'being a writer' (which is not the same as writing), I would have been discouraged when I looked at my family, so ordinary do they seem and so barren the outlook.

I scan the unfeatured landscape of my childhood and find no one the least bit larger than life, and a dearth of eccentricity. The only possible candidates to shove their noses above the horizon are my mother's

two sisters, Aunty Kathleen and Aunty Myra. They both of them marry late in life, and for most of my childhood are what they are pleased to call career girls. This actually means shop assistants, Aunty Kathleen working in Manfield's shoe shop on Commercial Street, Aunty Myra in White's, Ladies' Mantles on Briggate.

My aunties both like to think of themselves as good sports, vivacious and outgoing are the kind of adjective they aspire to and, to be fair to her, Aunty

Kath is always laughing, a big toothy laugh, her ridiculous attempts at gentility redeemed by a streak of coarseness.

Neither of them are what used to be called maiden aunts, though it is tacitly assumed that now they are in their forties they are unlikely to marry, particularly Aunty Kathleen whose role is to stay at home at Gilpin Place and look after Grandma. But neither of them are at all straitlaced and too vulgar often for my father, who hates anything that he calls cheeky, or 'off-colour remarks'. In this respect my mother is more like her sisters than he cares, for all the women who figure in my childhood markedly more vulgar than the men.

Both aunties are marathon talkers, Aunty Kathleen in particular, who after work often comes up home and regales us with all the news of her day selling shoes at Manfield's, told in Proustian detail. She talks with exaggerated care and correctness, her conversation punctuated by phrases like 'As it transpired,' 'If you take my meaning,' and 'If you follow me, Walter,' little verbal tugs intended to make sure her audience is still at her heels, following her down the track of some interminable, over-detailed and ultimately inconsequential narrative. Dad suffers this tedious saga with as good grace as he can muster, then, when the door finally closes behind her, he bursts out, 'I wouldn't care but you're no further on when she's finished.'

Both aunties are social climbers, albeit very much on the lower slopes. I've told the story before, but it is Aunty Kathleen who makes me aware that social pretension is a relative business. We are on a tram going down Wellington Road and passing the gasworks, when she lays a hand on my arm. 'Alan. That is the biggest gasworks in England. And I know the manager.'

Both aunties are social climbers, albiet very much on the lower slopes.

A different order of aunt is Aunt Eveline Peel, my grandmother's sister-in-law. Aunt Eveline is never Aunty Eveline. I suppose because she is older and too substantial for that. A pianist for the silent films, come the talkies she takes up housekeeping in Bradford, her employer a widower, a Mr Wilson, somebody big in the woollen trade who lives near Challow Dene.

Aunt Eveline speaks of Mr Wilson with exaggerated deference, but on the only occasion we are taken upstairs to meet him he turns out to be a small fat man who looks like a toad with immense circumferential flies that end halfway up his chest. He is smoking a huge cigar and looks like the capitalist in the cartoon. It's a shock when I realise that Aunt Eveline treats him with such respect because she wouldn't say no to becoming his second wife – an ambition that is never realised.

On the side, Aunt Eveline is a corsetière, fitting and selling corsets to a private clientèle on a freelance basis, a regular sideline of single ladies, particularly substantial ladies like Aunt Eveline, who plainly wear and therefore advertise the product they are marketing.

However, it is always dinned into my brother and me that we must never say Aunt Eveline is fat, or indeed mention anyone being fat in Aunt Eveline's presence, fatness a subject to be avoided altogether. Had size not been put on the agenda, as it were, it would never occur to either of us to say anything, because to say Aunt Eveline is fat implies that

... Fatness is a subject to be avoided altogether.

there is a possibility of her being something else, whereas to us, as children, her name and her shape are inseparable. She does, it's true, have an enormous bust and one which as a child actually confuses me about the nature of the female anatomy. Her breasts are so large as to make the cleavage between them seem like a dark and even mossy chasm. Aunt Eveline is wont to shield the entrance to this mysterious shaft with a lace-bordered frontal not unlike the antimacassars that grace the backs of Grandma's three-piece suite – between the back of the easy chair and the proud swell of Aunt Eveline's bust there not being much to choose. Half hidden though it is, this cleavage seems to my ten-year-old eyes so deep as to lead to a definite orifice, a kind of Gaping Gyll going down into the recesses of the body.

There's no evidence of such an orifice on the only naked woman I've seen, the frontispiece to our copy of *Everybody's Home Doctor*, but that she shows no trace of a pectoral vagina or an inter-mammary cleft does not entirely dispel the notion, which persists until the brink of adolescence when I happen to mention it to my brother, who puts paid to it with some scorn.

On Sundays, Aunt Eveline comes over from Bradford and there are musical evenings at Gilpin Place. The children are warned to keep back as a shovelful of burning coals from the kitchen range is carried smoking through the house to light the fire in

the sitting room, before we sit down to high tea in
the kitchen. After tea, we all adjourn and, the sitting
room still smelling of smoke, Aunt Eveline arranges
herself on the piano stool and with my father on the
violin ('Now then, Walter, what shall we give them?')
kicks off with a selection from *Glamorous Night*.
Then, having played themselves in, they accompany
Uncle George, my father's brother, in some songs.
Uncle George is a bricklayer and has a fine voice and
a face as red as his bricks. He sings 'Bless this House'
and 'Where'er You Walk', and sometimes Grandma
has a little cry.

Some Sundays, though, we are taken over to
Halifax to see Uncle Norris, Aunt Eveline's ne'er-do-
well brother, a dapper white-haired little man looking
a bit like Gandhi and now in a Halifax council home.
He is always eager, cheerful and over-talkative,
because he knows he is unlikely to be in the home for
long, nor any of the other inmates either. All will be
liberated and amply provided for once the world
acknowledges what he has been proclaiming for years,
namely that he, Norris Peel, has discovered the cure
for arthritis.

Uncle Norris's cure consists of cutting off the feet
of one's socks, thus going barefoot in one's shoes with

the rest of the sock worn simply as an anklet, secured to the foot by a piece of elastic running under the instep. This is how he wears his socks and since he doesn't suffer from arthritis, it must be a cure. That he has never had arthritis in the first place – nor anybody else in the family – doesn't occur to him. We are never there more than five minutes before he fetches out the dog-eared letter he has had from Mr Churchill's private secretary, taking note of his comments in which Mr Churchill, the letter says, has been most interested. Uncle Norris has written suggesting that his cut-off socks should be made standard equipment for all the armed forces and the fact that the country has emerged victorious in 1945 is proof that his advice must have been taken. Recognition can only be a matter of time.

Churchill is only one of the celebrities he has written to. Wilfred Pickles, Isobel Barnett, Semprini, a personality has scarcely to shove his or her nose above the horizon before Uncle Norris tries to enlist them in the no feet in the socks campaign. And his faith never falters. When he is

Churchill is only one of the celebrities he has written to.

already dying, he sends a letter promising us a share in the fortune he is about to inherit. He has discovered the existence in America of a multi-million-dollar research project into the cause of arthritis and has written telling them to abandon their research and just cut off the feet of their socks. Now he daily expects a reply in which they make over to him their entire endowment.

'He's batchy,' says Dad, meaning he's crazy but, as a child, I don't think Uncle Norris's ideas are particularly mad or even eccentric; they are only slightly more so than my aunties' insistence that we are descended from Sir Robert Peel, or my own thought, once voiced at Gilpin Place and briskly squashed by Dad, that Uncle Clarence, my mother's brother killed in the First War, might be the Unknown Soldier.

... they are only slightly more eccentric than my auntie's insistence that we are descended from Sir Robert Peel ...

I still have much of Aunt Eveline's music, albums covered in brown paper, the edges bound in brown paper too for easier turning over when in the darkened pit of the Electric, she gazes up at the silent screen while thumping out 'Any Time's Kissing Time', 'Mahbubah' or 'The Careless Cuckoo Cake Walk' by Ernest Bucalossi, in brackets 'very animated'.

Here is 'The Mosquito's Parade' by Howard Whitney, 'At the Temple Gates' by Gatty Sellars, and sheets and sheets of Ivor Novello. Every Sunday night she thumps out these old standards on the Gilpin Place piano, with occasional updates, 'Forgotten Dreams' by Leroy Anderson, the theme from *Limelight*, which I give her a few years or so before she dies.

But it isn't death that puts paid to these musical evenings, though when Aunt Eveline dies we inherit her piano and take it home. What takes its place in the smoky sitting room is a second-hand television set and it's this which, within a year or so, makes such musical evenings inconceivable. My other aunties don't mind, as talking has always had to be suspended while Aunt Eveline presides at the piano, whereas with the TV no one minds if you talk. And until they get a proper table for it, the TV even squats for a while in triumph on the piano stool that Aunt Eveline has occupied for so long.

Unsaid Prayers

ON THE AUGUST MORNING IN 1952 when I enlisted
in the York and Lancaster Regiment at Pontefract
Barracks, I was asked what religion I was and said C.
of E. This was not just a formal declaration as I was
at that time a practising Anglican, attending church
twice every Sunday, dutifully saying my prayers night
and morning, and had I been pressed about what these
days are called one's life-choices, I might well have said
that I was likely to end up either a librarian or a vicar.

Saying prayers is actually much on my mind on
this particular day as the sickly tableau of my kneeling
down by my barrack-room bed to the derision of my
fellow-conscripts has been one of several highly coloured
scenes with which I have been tormenting myself in the
months leading up to my conscription. To me at eight-
een, such ostentatious piety constitutes a real spiritual
hurdle and one that God, I feel, will be expecting me to
take. In his place I would be altogether more under-
standing, but this is one of the difficulties I have with
God: I am a much nicer and more sympathetic person
than I feel Him to be, who, despite his much advertised
love and compassion, I see as a close relative of what
William Empson called 'the omnipotent ferret'.

I lie there in my bed that night as the blizzard
of obscenity that has been going on all day gradually

dwindles and my comrades fall asleep; I wonder if
I were to get up in the dark and say my prayers
whether anyone would notice. Next moment it is
morning and all hell breaks loose again. Morning
prayers are out of the question. Round one, I feel, has
gone to God – the notion that God wants me to fail
always part of the trouble.

God hadn't troubled me unduly or I Him until
I was fourteen, when I am confirmed in the Church
of England and become for a time fervently religious.
This was a more common
stage for a boy to go
through then than it is
now, the change having as
much to do with the
diversification of leisure as
it does with the decline of

*... God hadn't
troubled me unduly
or I Him until I was
fourteen ...*

belief. In those days, most social life tends to centre
round the church and confirmation not only brings
you into full communion, it also procures you
membership of the youth club.

Then, too, one tends now to forget how smart
God was in the years during and immediately after the
war. C.S. Lewis remarked that, during the war, the
churches were as crowded as the cinema, and though

in the late forties and early fifties the cinema is definitely in the lead, the Almighty still keeps some of his chic. Auden is a member of the Church of England, T.S. Eliot and Christopher Fry are in the forefront of the drama, so to be an Anglican then is to be at culture's leading edge.

Whether I actually believe doesn't really come into it as, to its credit, the Church of England has never particularly bothered itself whether its members are saved or not, but I am also a member of another religious organisation that does. This is the Crusaders, an evangelical bible class, membership of which is confined to boys at public and grammar schools. What boys at council schools are supposed to do, I don't know. (Thank their stars, if they have any sense.) The Crusaders meet on Sunday afternoons in an upstairs room of a congregational church in Cumberland Road. The world having moved on, the church has since housed a Design Partnership, the upstairs room probably the computer, but I never pass the end of that road these days without looking up at those windows and regretting the blighted years when I went there Sunday by Sunday.

The bible class is run by a local auctioneer of great piety who, in the intervals of rousing hymns, drums into us impressionable schoolboys the wickedness of the world and how damned our souls are in it. But all this, he tells us, we can leave behind if only we will let Christ into our hearts. Many of the boys who attend Crusaders are more worldly wise than I am and take it all with a pinch of salt (and since the Crusaders also run summer camps on the Isle of Wight there is some spin off). But not me. Sunday by Sunday, I try to persuade myself that this apparently unmistakable experience of opening my heart to Christ has happened to me. But it hasn't. All that does happen is that I am tutored in a kind of intellectual dishonesty which enables me to pretend I am a different person than I am.

This is bad enough, but what the Crusaders also do is to convince me that I am wicked. I am not wicked, but it takes me another ten years to realise that I'd perhaps be a bit happier if I were. Years later, I read Edmund Gosse's masterpiece *Father and Son*, an account of his childhood blighted by fundamentalist religion, and found everything I had had so painfully to learn for myself set out there.

... what the Crusaders also do is to convince me that I am wicked.

At church, it might be thought my zeal would rejoice a vicar's heart and maybe it does, but actually I think the parish clergy find my fervour faintly embarrassing. A fervent Anglican is a bit of a contra-diction in terms anyway, but I am conscious that my constant presence at the Eucharist, often midweek as well as Sundays, is thought to be rather unhealthy. As the celebrant sallies forth from the vestry on a cold winter's morning and finds me sitting or getting in a spot of silent prayer, he must feel a bit like a doctor opening the surgery door and discover-ing the sole occupant of the waiting room some tiresome hypo-chondriac (I am that too actually). Shy, awkward and innocent of the world, I know I am a disappointment to the clergy. What they want are brands to pluck from the burning and that is not me by a long chalk; I'd never even been near the fire.

Shy, awkward and innocent of the world, I know that I am a disappoint-ment to the clergy.

Those early morning services with just a handful of regulars in the side chapel, the others generally maiden ladies who had famously cycled there on tall bicycles through the autumn mists, are to me the true stuff of religion, the real taste of God. But though I do not admit it myself, I know that what the clergy prefer are occasions like Christmas Eve when the church is packed to the doors. For many in the congregation this is their one visit to church in the year. Plumping to my knees with split-second timing, I scornfully note how few of these festive communicants know the service and certainly not backwards like I do. Most of them don't even kneel but sit, head in hand as if they are on the lavatory, this their one spiritual evacuation of the year.

Even though I attend so regularly, I'm always nervous of drinking from the chalice at Holy Communion lest I catch something. At the sparsely attended Eucharists on a normal Sunday there's not much risk of infection as one can bank on finding oneself at the communion rail alongside a person of proven piety and blameless life. As my turn comes for the chalice, it's true I may think of the TB or cancer I might catch from my neighbour, but come the Christmas Watch Night service these minor ailments are forgotten. Then, in my mind, it is VD that is the bugbear. Christmas, that joyous festival of the Christian year, figures in my calendar as a fearful health hazard. With the church chock-a-block with

publicans and sinners, one never knows who is going
to be one's drinking companion. It is all my mother's
fault. She has brought us up never to share a lemon-
ade bottle with other boys, and wiping the top with
your hand, she said, was no protection, so I know the
dainty dab with the napkin the priest gives the chalice
makes no difference at all. There is God, of course,
in whose omnipotence I am supposed to believe:
He might run to some mystical antisepsis, but then He
might not. That I should catch syphilis from the chalice
might be all part of His
plan. The other place I am
frightened of contracting
it is, of course, from the
seat of the public lavatory,
and that the rim of the
toilet should be thus linked
with the rim of the chalice is also part of the wonderful
mystery of God. It is on such questions of hygiene
rather than any of theology that my faith cuts its
teeth. I see myself walking back from the altar and
plunging to my knees, then, at the first opportunity,
surreptitiously spitting into my handkerchief. But I
know that if God had marked me down for VD and a
test of faith, no amount of spitting is going to help. It

*That I should catch
syphilis from the
chalice might be all
part of His plan.*

is all chickenfeed to the Ancient of Days.

This religion or religiosity survives the army and persists well into my twenties. I am still gabbling some kind of prayers when I am at university and one of the most acutely shaming moments of my life is when another undergraduate catches me at it.

Still I have never regretted that time. The only literary work I know large chunks of by heart is the Book of Common Prayer. I have a bad memory, but these days the words still come welling up from that damp unvisited cellar where they were laid down all those years ago. And if the service happens to be something like Compline, which has not yet been pedestrianised, that is fine. But most of the services now are not as I remember them. They have been modernised, demystified, so that to go into a church nowadays knowing the Book of Common Prayer is about as helpful as going into a disco knowing the veleta.

Thinking of religion now, I wish I had been better at it, but looking back on it, particularly in my boyhood, I can see that it was a way of rationalising the fact that I was awkward and shy, and for a time I even thought I would enter the priesthood, though not for any better reason than that I looked like a vicar. A few years later, when I had started wearing glasses, I nearly became a don on the same dubious principle. This is not as silly as it sounds. People often end up doing what the mirror tells them they are suited for, while feeling themselves quite different inside, and in the process whole lifetimes are thrown away.

No Mean City

TO HAVE BEEN BORN AND BROUGHT UP in a northern provincial city seemed in those days more of a handicap than an inheritance. 'How,' I think at the time, 'how will I ever get out of here? Who in this place has ever come to anything?' And (a question that has cropped up from time to time since): 'Where is Life?'

In those days the answer to that seemed to be Down South, capital D, capital S, certainly not in the West Riding, dark rainy, ringed by mills and wild moors. And if not Down South then the North and East Ridings seem more of a promised land if only because life there is a bit more up my imaginary street.

Go east of Leeds and certainly beyond York, and there are smiling cottages round village greens, duck ponds and even the occasional thatched roof with only the busy red buses of the West Yorkshire Road Car Co. (terminus on Wellington Street opposite the Central Station) to remind one that this is home still, and mucky Leeds not far off. Past York there is a prospect of distant hills and sunlit uplands (Herriot country these days and home of *Heartbeat*) and then the moors you crossed to get to Whitby or Scarborough. In other ridings than ours there are soaring churches and grand gateways into great parks that promise Palladian houses and glimpses of that storybook world that as a child I always hanker after.

Leeds, though, is different and it is being brought up in a city that is almost entirely of the nineteenth century that makes me, as a boy, famished for antiquity and long to get away from Leeds so that I can find some.

What I do not appreciate, though, is how deeply the city puts its stamp on me. No child brought up in Leeds or any large provincial city, can help but be aware that his or her life is under-pinned and overseen by the Corporation. The arms of the City of Leeds are embossed on public library books and on the exercise books we write in at school; they are emblazoned on the side of the trams and on the dustcarts; any public celebration sees medallions with the arms of the city fixed to lamp-posts and public buildings and even strung across the streets in the city centre. There was – and it's still there – a coat of arms fixed to the wrought-iron tracery over the entrance to the City Markets in Kirkgate; another more battered one survives over the Headrow

What I do not appreciate, though, is how deeply the city puts its stamp on me.

entrance to what was then the Police Department and City Reference Library. The arms could even be found growing in Roundhay Park where, together with the Floral Clock, the owl and the lamb are painstakingly planted out in alyssum and lobelias by the Corporation Parks department.

Thus it is that a child is reminded of the identity of the city at every turn much as – and I don't think the comparison is fanciful – a fifteenth-century citizen of Florence or Venice was reminded in the same way.

This presence of the Corporation in our lives is constant and largely benevolent. A reasonable performance in Higher School Certificate or any acceptance by a university, means, for instance, that a boy or girl is automatically awarded a scholarship by the city. Slightly better results produce a scholarship from the state, but the city educates its own and any award by a college or university, art school, drama school or whatever, is topped up as a matter of course by the Corporation Education Department, with its imposing offices opposite the side door of the Town Hall in Calverley Street.

The effect of this continuing Corporation presence is to instil even in the most heedless of its children a sense of belonging. And it isn't the same as

the windy stuff about pride in the school that we are regularly regaled with at Morning Assembly; no one takes that seriously for a moment. But it is a kind of pride, and though one wouldn't have wanted to think so or be told so then, a boy or girl nurtured in Leeds or Bradford or Manchester has some sense of being a son or daughter of a solid self-confident city and that when, in due course, one went away as I did to university, the sense of being still part of the city, like it or not, is in one's baggage.

And, of course, for me and most of my schoolfellows everything we have in the way of education has been provided for us free of charge. My education – elementary school, secondary school, university – costs my parents nothing, their only sacrifice (which they don't see as a sacrifice) that by staying on at school beyond sixteen, I'm not bringing in a wage. Education in its wider sense is free too. The libraries are free, open every day except Sunday from nine in the morning until eight at night; the art gallery is free, the museums; even symphony concerts are virtually free – a school ticket to sit behind the orchestra in 1950 costing 6d.

The rightness and appropriateness of this is not questioned by either of the political parties on the City Council – though the orchestra which is less generally acceptable, is starved of funds by both. So much, though, we take for granted, and in my view rightly – it being, it seems to me, the mark of a civilised society that certain privileges should be taken for granted such as education, health care and the safety to walk the streets (and to have pleasant streets to walk in). Though there is much that irritates, saddens and angers me about Leeds and what has happened to it since, I shall always be grateful for what I was given there. And so when, particularly in the eighties, one found a different so-called philosophy prevailing, namely that people properly value only what they pay for, I remember my growing up in Leeds and what we were given then, and want none of it.

... I shall always be grateful for what I was given there.

To find much of that thinking now embraced by the Labour Party, in particular where education is concerned, is especially bitter. Of course, it has to be paid for; but to say 'Education has to be paid for,' and 'The students must pay for it,' is not the same thing.

As I say, my parents paid not a penny for my education, but had they been told that in order to go to university I must take out a loan, however reasonably it could be re-paid, so strong is their fear of debt that I would not have been allowed to go, nor, I'm sure, would many of my contemporaries. I would be surprised if this is not the case still in many households today and I think it is wrong.

... so strong is their fear of debt that I would not have been allowed to go.

Of course, I keep saying that our education was free, though there is a sense in which it was not free at all, as it had already been paid for by what had been withheld from our parents and grandparents, packed, in Larkin's words, into:

> ... close-ribbed streets [that] rise and fall,
> Like a great sigh out of the last century.
> (*The Building*)

Our education was not free; it was owing. It was our

birthright because it had not been theirs. Now I am not sure anyone has a birthright or knows what a birthright means.

The proud municipal tradition I have been talking about has gone; began to crumble I suppose in the sixties when the great provincial cities started to tear themselves apart in the name of profit and redevelopment, so that by the end of the seventies one place looked very much like another.

Long since gone are those permanent officials whose names never seemed to change throughout my childhood and youth: George Guest, the Director of Education, W. Vane Morland, the Director of Transport, R.A.H. Livett, the Director of Housing, names that I remember and which I see Leeds-born Keith Waterhouse, slightly older than I am, remembers too. They were the municipal pillars of my youthful Leeds world, their names as constant and unchanging as Tyrrell of Avon, the film censor whose certificate preceded every film one ever saw; or H.O. Peppiatt, the Secretary of the Bank of England, whose signature authenticated every note – grand and

... by the end of the seventies one place looked very much like another.

mysterious personalities who peopled one's childhood through endless years the same.

The downfall of these municipal great men was handily symbolised when, in an architectural salvage warehouse in Elland, in 1988, I saw stacked up the fixtures and fittings from the Leeds Corporation Education Department building. So the panelling that used to deck out the office of the redoubtable George Guest, to whom I and many others of my age owe our education, now graces some converted barn in Wensleydale or kits out some modish design consultancy canalside.

The accent of course doesn't seem to change – a Leeds accent not at all rough-sounding to me but rather wet and lackadaisical. I tried to lose my northern accent at one period, the fifties I suppose, when the provincial voice was still looked down on. Then it came back and now I don't know where I am, sometimes saying my 'a's long, sometimes short, though it's the 'u's that are a continuing threat – words

… I tried to lose my northern accent at one period, the fifties I suppose, when the provincial voice was still looked down on.

like butcher, study, sugar, and names like 'Cutbush' always lying in ambush.

Once in the seventies at Cambridge I did a recital with Judi Dench, northern herself but from York which is rather different. I had to read a passage by Goldsmith about Garrick:

> He cast off friends as a huntsman his pack
> For he knew when he pleas'd he could whistle
>   them back.
> Of praise a mere glutton he swallow'd what
>   came
> And [here it comes] *the puff of a dunce* he
>   mistook it for fame.

On the night in question I had to have two stabs at it: the first time it came out as 'the paff of a dunce', the second time as 'the poof of a dance', thereby, I'm sure, causing a good deal of pain to Dadie Rylands, one of the last survivors of Bloomsbury, who was directing the proceedings. Dame Judi didn't help by openly giggling. The truth is anyone from the north who ventures south of the Trent contracts an incurable disease of the vowels; it's a disease to which weather forecasters are particularly prone, and, for some reason, lecturers in sociology.

ALAN BENNETT is one of Britain's best-loved and most highly acclaimed writers. He has written widely for radio, television and theatre. His latest play, *The History Boys*, won several awards, including *Evening Standard* and Critics' Circle Awards for Best Play and the Laurence Olivier Award for Best New Play. It also won six Tony Awards, including Best Play, following an extremely successful transfer to Broadway. In 2006 Bennett was named Author of the Year at the British Book Awards for *Untold Stories*, his recent collection of memoirs and diaries.

Also available from BBC Books

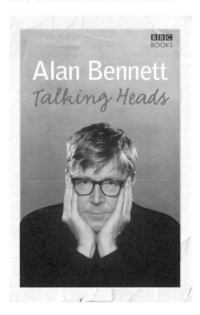